Samuel the Lamanite

written by Tiffany Thomas
illustrated by Nikki Casassa

CFI · An imprint of Cedar Fort, Inc. · Springville, Utah

HARD WORDS:
Samuel, Jesus, years

PARENT TIP: Explain that "q" almost always is paired with the letter "u" in a word.

This is Samuel.

Samuel is a
man of God.

Samuel is a
good Lamanite.

Some of the Nephites are now bad.

Samuel stands on a big wall.

Samuel tells the
Nephites that
Jesus will be
born in five years.

The bad Nephites are mad.

They try to
hurt Samuel.

9

Samuel runs away.

Some Nephites are baptized
and are now good.

The good
Nephites wait
for Jesus
to be born.

The end.

ISBN 13: 978-1-4621-4337-5

Published by CFI, an imprint of Cedar Fort, Inc. • 2373 W. 700 S., Suite 100, Springville, UT 84663
Distributed by Cedar Fort, Inc., www.cedarfort.com

Cover design and interior layout design by Shawnda T. Craig
Cover design © 2022 Cedar Fort, Inc.
Printed in China • Printed on acid-free paper
10 9 8 7 6 5 4 3 2 1